THE OFFICIAL
I HATE CATS BOOK

THE OFFICIAL
I HATE CATS BOOK

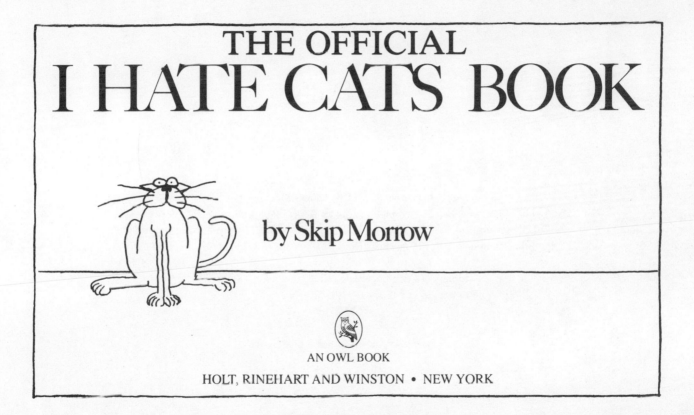

by Skip Morrow

AN OWL BOOK

HOLT, RINEHART AND WINSTON • NEW YORK

For Duffy

Library of Congress Catalog Card Number: 80-81251
ISBN: 0-03-057708-X
First Edition

Printed in the United States of America
1   3   5   7   9   10   8   6   4   2

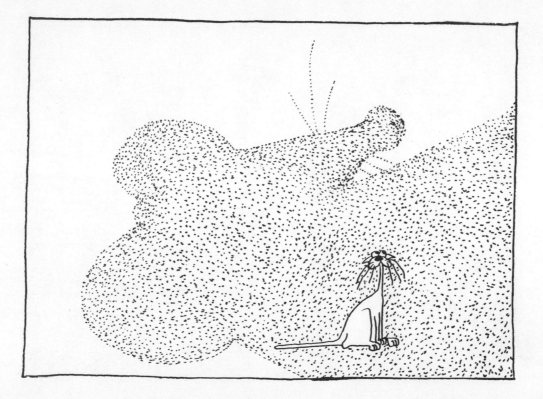

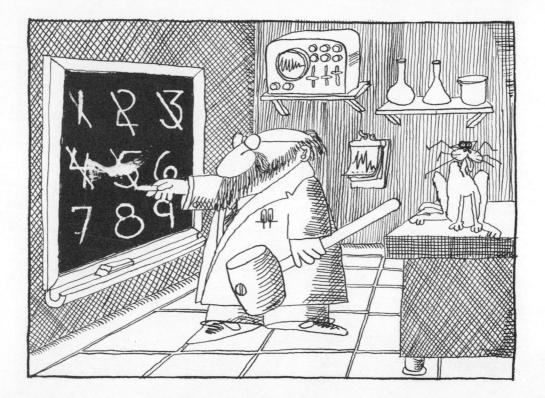

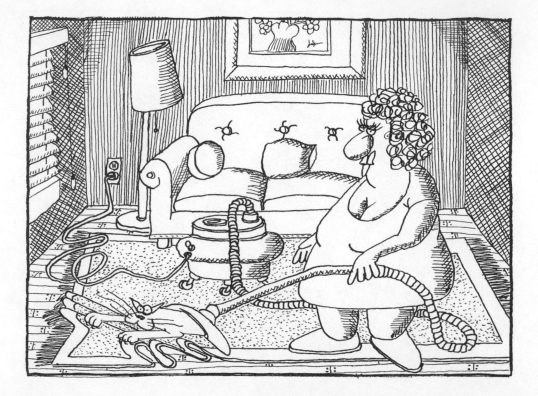

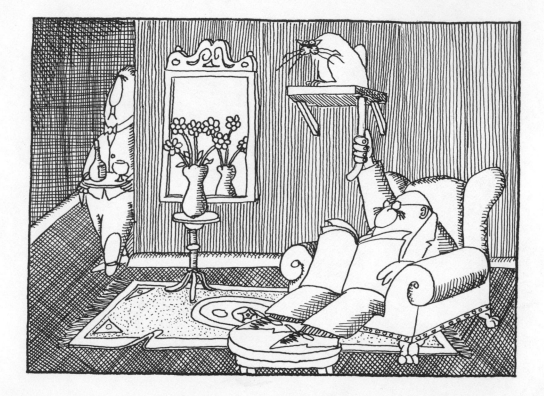

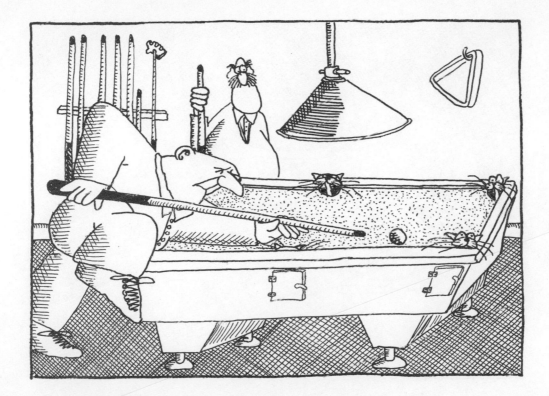

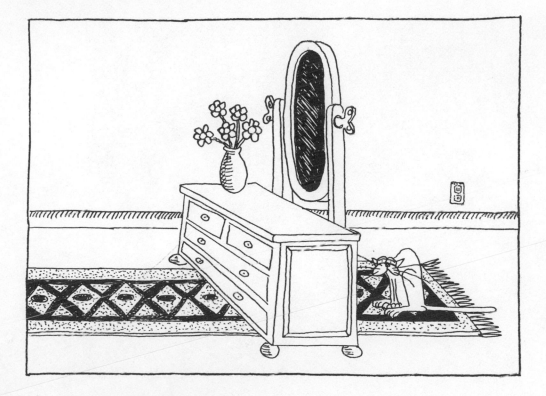

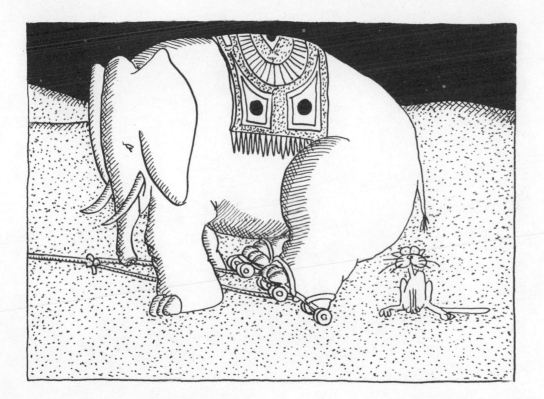

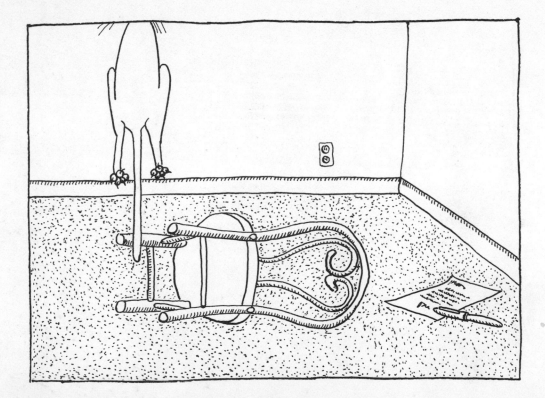